Anger

A
POSITIVE
ENERGY

Adele J. Gonzalez, D.Min.

Editor: Fernando R. Senra
Cover Design: JMGD, Inc.
Design & Diagramming: Manuel Villaverde

All Bible quotes taken from the New Revised Standard Version

Copyright © October, 2004, Get-With-It, LLC.
All rights reserved

ISBN 0-9761639-0-X

Published by Get-With-It, LLC.

Printed by Nu Press of Miami, Inc.
Miami, Florida

Dedication

To *Peco* and *Diana*
who believed in my gift
and have walked with me
every step of the way.

Contents

INTRODUCTION

For over 25 years I have worked with individuals and groups in secular and religious settings who wish to enjoy healthier and more successful interpersonal relationships. One of the issues constantly surfacing is that of anger, a powerful emotion often interfering with the individual and communal well being.

After the terrorist attacks of September 11, 2001, the war in Iraq, the scandals in the Roman Catholic Church and the growing tension between the United States and other countries, many people feel frustrated by the senseless loss of lives and the fear that the national economy will not improve anytime soon. Many have lost their trust in governments, corporations and even religious institutions and are left feeling powerless against an abundance of conflict and confusing information.

I have discovered that offering seminars and retreats on dealing with anger is one response to the needs of people today. Invariably, after each of these gatherings, participants ask me what they can do to continue this process by themselves or with friends and relatives when they return home. This book is the response to those requests.

The book is divided into four chapters that follow the order of the presentations, and is equally suited to individual use or group process. It is not necessary to have attended the seminar or retreat in order to benefit from this book.

Chapter one explains the emotion of anger along with its causes. Chapter two examines the negative effects of anger when it is ignored or denied. Chapter three suggests three positive outcomes of this powerful emotion when we befriend it. Chapter four provides concrete suggestions for readers to continue exploring the positive energy of the emotion of anger. Throughout the book, I will suggest exercises to help at that particular point of the process.

I hope that you will benefit from reading this book as much as I have from writing it.

Adele J. Gonzalez
September 27, 2004

CHAPTER ONE

Understanding Anger

"Anger *n. distress, sorrow... a feeling of displeasure resulting from injury, mistreatment, opposition, etc."*
—Webster's Dictionary

Feelings

Feelings are important tools to know ourselves. They point out situations that cause us pleasure or pain so that we learn to distinguish how our environment and relationships affect us. They tell us that we are alive! Yet, most people are uncomfortable with their feelings especially when they are considered "negative", as in the case of anger.

The word anger has the same Latin root as *angustia* (anguish) and *angina* (spasmodic suffocation). In both cases we do not place any value judgment on the feelings themselves and take them for what they are: signals telling us that something is wrong in our lives or our health. Why then do we treat anger differently?

The notion that feelings can be "good or bad" comes from the ways in which we see them expressed. When people refer to anger as a negative emotion, they speak of the violent acts meant to fight back at the supposed cause of the frustration; actions that are difficult to handle and have the potential to harm ourselves and others. These violent outbursts of rage in which self-control is lost have given a bad reputation to the emotion of anger in our society.

In the case of those who have been raised in the Christian tradition, strong feelings can be the cause of unhealthy guilt. We have been taught that certain emotions "should not" be welcomed. Our consciousness has been programmed by parents, clergy and society in general to believe that "we should not feel this or that". Nevertheless, we know that feelings are *amoral*, that is, in and of themselves they are neither right nor wrong. The important thing is what we do with our feelings and how we express them.

Anger ranks at the top of the list of those emotions that are labeled "negative" or even "sinful." Oftentimes as children we were scolded for being angry. This meant being punished for our display of negative or destructive behavior. This "angry" response to our actions has caused most of us to confuse our feelings with the way in which we express them.

As you follow the process outlined in this book you will identify the role that anger plays in your life now and how you can tap into its positive energy to gradually move from a place of pain and stagnation to a place of growth and freedom.

Before you do the exercises…

If you are using this book in a group context, I suggest you stay with the same partner or small group for the duration of the process.

I also recommend keeping a personal journal. In every exercise in this book I provide enough space for you to write. The purpose of recording your answers is to offer you a place where you can identify and hopefully understand what is happening in your life. Journaling goes beyond recording events. It is a tool for a deeper reflection on who you are and how you are responding to life's events. If you are a person of faith, you will also discover who you are in relationship to your God and the ways in which God is working in your life. In any case, journaling is a freeing discipline because there is no "right" way of doing it.

Exercise 1: Personal Reflection

Begin by getting in touch with your own feelings. Take a few minutes by yourself to answer the following questions as honestly as possible:

1. What makes you angry? Write down the first three things that come to your mind.

- _____

_____

_____

_____

_____

_____

_____

_____

_____

_____

_____

-

-

2. How do you usually express your anger? (Check all that apply)

a) ___ Using sarcasm.

b) ___ Throwing or breaking things.

c) ___ Getting sick.

d) ___ Becoming physically or verbally abusive.

e) ___ Crying.

f) ___ Going for a walk or a run.

g) ___ Becoming totally silent for a long time.

h) ___ _____.

i) ___ _____.

j) ___ _____.

Take a few minutes to review your answers. What do they tell you about your anger or the way in which you express it?

If you are in a group, share your responses in dyads or in groups of four.

Anger

Before you attempt to analyze or evaluate your answers, let us look at what anger is. Simply put, anger is a reaction to your frustration because your ideal or expectations are not being satisfied. If you are like most people, you have strong opinions about the way people or things "should be". You expect a lot from your spouse, friends, children, parents, job, church, and even from yourself. This is normal and even desirable. Ideals move us to affect change when necessary, to right wrongs and to dream dreams. The problem is that more often than not you encounter a wide gap between your expectations and reality. This gap causes a frustration which varies in degrees depending on the severity of the gap and the importance of the ideal.

Imagine this situation: You enter a supermarket to pick up some lunch on your way to work. You not only find a long waiting line, but the person in front of you does not have a valid ID card to show the cashier. She calls the manager who, of course, is busy in another part of the store. The light above the register continues to blink as you feel your blood beginning to boil. You are frustrated and rightly so. In normal circumstances, this feeling is temporary and disappears as soon as the inconvenience is resolved. Nothing to worry about!

When this frustration is experienced repeatedly, caused by serious abuses, injustices or betrayal, eventually it will turn into anger. At that point, the intensity of the feeling has surpassed that of a simple, occasional inconvenience.

I compare anger with a cellular phone. It rings because someone is calling me and the ring is trying to get my attention. There is no evil intention in the phone. In itself it is only a medium to deliver a message. Analogically, anger is a ring, a bell that tells me that I need to pay attention to someone or something; there is a message for me and I better answer it. When I do not answer, I may feel better, but eventually I will be more frustrated when, at the end of the day, my voice mail informs me that I have 15 unheard messages. It would be ludicrous to get upset at my cellular and throw it against the wall. This may stop the ringing temporarily, but will not take away the people who are trying to contact me. If they do not get me by phone, they will try other means to make themselves heard.

Just as in the case of the cellular phone, my anger is notifying me that I need to pay attention to my frustration which has gone unattended for some time. At this point I can do one of two things:

1.- Ignore it, smash it against the wall or remove the battery so it does not bother me anymore.

2.- Answer and listen to the message it brings.

Exercise 2: To answer or not to answer

Review your answers to Exercise 1. Question #2: "How do you usually express anger?" Compare your behavior with the list of reactions to the cell phone example explained above.

Do you:

    a) pay attention to the ringing?

    b) ignore it and pretend it is not there?

    c) break it so it does not work anymore?

    d) silence it by removing the battery?

Take a few minutes to write your reflections or to share them with your group or partner.

Hopefully, you are becoming more aware of what the emotion of anger really is: a sign, a wake up call, a ring indicating that something is going wrong in you and that it needs immediate attention!

Use the following chart to see how anger develops:

Remember that anger is simply an amoral strong emotion that arises in response to an ongoing frustration, but because of the negative behaviors usually associated with it, anger has been maligned and placed in the list of undesirable and even "sinful" feelings. Particularly among Christians, the quest for perfection usually includes eliminating anger as an emotion.

As you continue this process, remember that this feeling is your friend and that there is nothing wrong with it!

CHAPTER TWO

When we ignore the ring

Pay attention.
The voice is coming from within you.

Let us now look at some of the negative behaviors that occur when we "do not answer the cell phone" and anger is ignored.

Trying to ignore the ring will not work simply because it is our own voice that it carries. That voice will continue to shout until we pay attention to it. When anger is ignored, denied or masked it has the potential to destroy us. The following chart illustrates this:

When anger is ignored it will turn into

⇩

Aggression / Violence

This aggression can be outwardly directed or inwardly directed.
Outwardly directed aggression does violence to others.
Inwardly directed aggression does violence to you.

Outwardly directed

active	*passive*
physical violence	passive aggression
verbal abuse	silence
gossip	indifference

Inwardly directed

active	*passive*
suicide	depression
addictions	illnesses

Outwardly directed aggression.

The emotion of anger is loaded with energy. When this energy is not owned and channeled properly it will become manifested in the form of aggression. It is the "pressure cooker" effect. The water is boiling and if it does not find an outlet, it will explode in our faces! Aggression, conscious or unconscious, is an attempt to let some of the steam out.

Perhaps the most easily identifiable form of aggression is *physical violence*. When we see someone hitting someone else, banging their fists against the wall, throwing or breaking things we surmise that they are angry. Actually, they are beyond anger and into its unhealthy expression which I am calling aggression or violence. As I have said earlier, it is this manifestation, along with verbal abuse, that has given anger its bad reputation.

Verbal abuse includes screaming at others and insulting or diminishing them with our words and gestures. This is also an unhealthy way of dealing with anger. Although verbal abuse is more acceptable in our society than physical violence, it is equally harmful and vicious. I have heard people excuse themselves by claiming to have a "loud voice" or be very "passionate", but that they do not mean any offense. These are lame excuses for an unjustifiable behavior. Once the abusive words have been put out there, it is impossible to take them back!

Gossip is the least recognizable form of outward violence. Because it does not include yelling or external aggressive behavior it tends to be accepted as part of the human condition. Gossip is as violent as hitting someone. We use our tongue to destroy a person's reputation behind his/her back. Gossip is not constructive criticism or friendly correction; it is cunning and two-faced and must be accepted for what it is, a devious form of violence.

The gossiper is usually motivated by envy or strong dislike of another person. When we hold someone else responsible for our misery or wish we could have what they have, we wish to hurt them in some way. By tarnishing their image and raising suspicion about their conduct we hope to get even. Gossip is foolish, unhealthy, and does not do anyone any good.

Other forms of violence are passive and more difficult to identify. The most common is accurately called *passive aggression*. When this behavior occurs, anger is disguised and the person maintains a self-image of serenity and non-violence. Passive aggressive persons are very difficult to deal with since they are not motivated to change. This form of violence affects not only relationships, but also performance. It is often manifested as persistent social or occupational ineffectiveness such as procrastination, forgetfulness or intentional inefficiency.

Passive aggressive behavior occurs everyday and destroys relationships. Take this example:

Susan and Richard have been married for 10 years. They love each other, but do not communicate well. For a long time Susan has felt hurt by what she perceives as Richard's indifference. He is always busy with work and not interested in home and family issues. Susan has tried to talk about her feelings, but Richard puts her off because he is too worried about the demands of his job.

Susan's hurt and frustration are turning into anger! A month ago, during breakfast, she "gave it to him", and told him how angry she felt. Richard claimed to be late for an important meeting and remarked that Susan was making a mountain out of an ant hill. He suggested that she call her sister and go shopping. Susan was furious and unknown to her the steam of her anger came out in the form of passive aggressive behavior.

For two weeks she has not been home when Richard arrives from work, dinner is never ready, but she insists that she is following his suggestion to go shopping with her sister and that this is making her feel much better. Last Saturday they were supposed to go to a concert for which they had bought tickets three months earlier. At the last minute when they were getting ready to leave, Susan developed a severe migraine headache and refused to attend the concert. Richard was frustrated, and surprisingly, his frustration did not make Susan feel any better.

Their inability to communicate had taken a turn

for the worse. *Passive aggression* had become a secret guest in their relationship!

Alongside passive aggression are *silence* and *indifference*. Both are very subtle ways to let the steam out and "hurt" others without becoming overtly violent. The *cold shoulder treatment*, the "*I am sorry, but I forgot*", and the *persistent tardiness*, are insidious ways to try to control a situation or a person who has failed to meet our expectations. It is aggression in a gala outfit!

EXERCISE 3: Where is your steam going?

Remember the image of the pressure cooker? If your steam is outwardly directed, you must be burning someone! Reflect on the italicized forms of aggression listed above. Do you relate to any of those behaviors? Have you ever experienced what Susan and Richard are going through?

● Is your steam going out in the form of:

        ___ Physical violence?

        ___ Verbal abuse?

        ___ Gossip?

        ___ Passive aggression?

        ___ Silent treatment?

        ___ Indifference?

● Be honest with yourself. No one can do this work for you…

1.- What are you getting out of this behavior? How is it of help to you? Are you changing anything or anyone with your actions?

2.- Do you think it may be time for you to move from this place of violence and stagnation to a place of peace and growth?

If you are working with a partner or in a small group, share only as much information as you feel comfortable with.

Inwardly directed aggression.

When the steam of the "pressure cooker" does not have an external outlet, the aggression boils inside and we "burn" ourselves. The frustration, the anger, and finally the violence turn inward, either actively or passively.

Suicide is the most destructive of the *inwardly directed active aggression.* The Center for Disease Control (CDC) lists the following as factors for suicide: feelings of hopelessness, aggressive tendencies, losses (relational, social, work or financial), physical illness, family history of child abuse and isolation, or the feeling of being cut off from other people. Although risk factors are not necessarily the causes of suicide, they increase the likelihood that persons will harm themselves. *Suicide* can be seen as a way to take control by removing ourselves from a painful situation. When we feel trapped and unable to break free from whatever is enslaving us, we may resort to suicide as a way to break free from our prison. Unfortunately, we may not even be aware of what caused the painful frustration in the first place.

Suicide is becoming common even among people who do not suffer from serious mental illnesses. Two of the groups most susceptible to this inner aggression are the young and the elderly. For both, the future appears uncertain and the present confusing, stressful or depressing. This can lead them to see suicide as a "solution", a way out of their pain without "hurting anyone". Guilt, low self-esteem and many other factors play important roles in this destructive and sad behavior.

Self-destruction can express itself through *addiction to drugs, alcohol, food, sex, work, gambling, etc.* The pattern is the same even when the actions differ. Many of us do not make the connection between these behaviors and anger. It is outside of the scope of this book to study the causes of addiction. I will limit myself to say that even in cases where there is a chemical disposition to addiction, dealing with anger in a healthy manner can help prevent many of its destructive outcomes.

Finally, one of the most harmful ways of directing our aggression inwardly is *depression*. There is not just one cause for depression. It is a complex condition that can occur as a result of many factors. In this book I am not referring to the depression caused by medications, genetic factors or mental illness. Here I am dealing primarily with the depression caused by the loss of a loved one, conflict with a family member, any kind of abuse, changing jobs, graduating, retiring, getting married or divorced, or after being diagnosed with a serious illness. (This is a sample list)

Similar to *suicide* and *addiction*, *depression* is an unconscious intra-punitive way of dealing with the frustration, the stress and the pain caused by events that we cannot control. It is our way of saying, "Stop the world, I want to get out!" We are unable to enjoy the things and relationships we once did and feel tired most of the time. Our sleep patterns and eating habits change and *if depression goes unattended it can lead to suicide.*

More common forms of *inwardly directed passive aggression are illnesses that do not have an apparent physical cause. Headaches, stomach disorders and many other symptoms* reflect a deeper reality: something is upsetting us. We are unhappy with the reality of our lives and we have neglected to answer the angry cell phone that has been ringing and ringing trying to get our attention. These *psychosomatic symptoms* seem to affect women more than men, maybe because overt aggressive behavior is not socially acceptable for "good, decent and educated women".

EXERCISE 4:
Is it worth what anger is doing to you?

How do you feel after reading the italicized forms of hurting yourself listed in the preceding section? Are you suffering from any of the intra-punitive violence that I just described?

Maybe you are not even aware of what is causing you to act this way. Try to go beyond the surface and identify the people or events that made you feel hurt to begin with. Do not let this moment of growth pass. Be honest with yourself!

If you decide to move from this place of pain and stagnation to a place of peace and freedom, what would that mean? Would there be any changes in your life? If so, what changes?

30

If you are working with a partner or in a small group, share only as much information as you feel comfortable with.

CHAPTER THREE

When we answer the cell phone

"You think you are alive because you breathe air? Shame on you, that you are alive in such a limited way. Don't be without Love, so you won't feel dead. Die in Love and stay alive forever."
    –Rumi

Hopefully, you are now willing to answer the cell phone. We have seen that ignoring the ring is not in our best interests, so we choose to look at anger face to face and allow it to talk to us. What will we hear when we listen to this powerful emotion?

First of all, we will discover that the emotion itself is friendly, it is actually "on our side", telling us that something is not right in our lives. Moreover, anger and disagreements are normal parts of healthy relationships and without them there is no growth. But it is good to remember that anger begins as a response to a perceived hurt or injustice by a situation that is not the way we think it should be, or a person who does not treat us the way we would like. Thus, anger begins with us, we are the authors of our own anger. No one has the power to make us feel angry; we must own it!

I like to think that, in this sense, anger is my friend, a companion in my journey calling me to growth and health.

Once we befriend our anger and open the lines of communication, we need to pay close attention to its message. For this, I suggest the use of the three well known steps of social analysis: seeing, judging and acting.

1.- **Seeing.** In this first step we gather the data.

What is going on in your life? Who or what is the target of your anger? Where is the steam going? Remember there is no moral judgment attached to the emotion only to your actions. Hopefully, the four previous exercises have helped you to answer these questions. During this part of the process, try to be patient and compassionate with yourself and others. Putting yourself down or playing the blame game will not be of any help.

2.- **Judging.** In this second step we analyze and evaluate.

Try to interpret the message that anger is trying to give you. You need wisdom for this. What are the specific causes of your anger? Is it the way your spouse treats you? Is it the incompetence of your employees or the insensitivity of your employer? Are you unhappy with your own performance? Keep in mind that often the initial frustration did not occur recently and you have been feeding this anger for a long time.

If this step is not handled with care, analyzing may do more harm than good. Take your time; you may even need to continue this process on a later day.

36

3.- **Acting**. In this third step we choose how we want to respond.

Seeing and judging do not make any sense unless we have the courage to act. If our anger goes unattended it will lead to threats or violence, and hurting ourselves or others are not desirable components of any relationship.

Now is the moment to start looking for healthy ways to deal with your anger. This process of reflection and action is ongoing and often difficult and painful. Do not try to rush it. In the following section I am offering three positive actions, but before you consider them, write your own ideas about this third step.

Positive actions.

Once you have a sense of what causes your anger and how you have been dealing with it, it is time to take healthier steps to channel it. I am offering three possible ways to claim the positive energy that this loaded emotion is offering you.

EXERCISE 5:
Option #1. Re-evaluate your expectations.

Often we expect from people what is humanly impossible to give. We want others to be perfect, loving and understanding. We bring such high expectations to our relationships that they are doomed to failure before they even begin.

Christians believe that human beings have an insatiable desire for love and divinity because they have been created in the image and likeness of God. If this is so, and I believe it is, then we are always searching for the divine in the form of love, beauty, joy, peace and goodness all around us. In my many years of experience I can attest to this principle. We try to fill that space with wealth, power or status, but the more we have, the more we seem to need. Nothing is enough to make us happy, nothing can satisfy the "longing". I have seen relationships destroyed because one party expected perfection and divinity from the other. In cases like these, frustration will set in sooner or later and it will eventually turn into anger. It is hard for some people to accept that they have caused their own anger by setting unrealistic expectations of each other.

Let us look at your own situation. If your pressure cooker is already boiling this is not the time to ignore your anger! You need to find positive ways to channel the energy within you.

40

Examine your expectations honestly. Realize that people or organizations are limited human beings and imperfect structures and that they cannot always give you what you ask of them.

Can you be more realistic about what you expect from others? How about from yourself? Are you suffering from *"acute perfectionitis"*?

Re-thinking your expectations and maybe modifying them takes wisdom and courage. This can be a long and difficult process especially if you have valued them most of your life.

- Changing your expectations does not mean:

    Giving in

    Giving up

    Failing

    Being weak

    Losing

- Being able to adjust your expectations to your reality without compromising what is right and just makes you a:

    better person

    happier person

    healthier person

    more successful person

    more productive person

    person at peace with him / herself

Spend as much time as you need reflecting on this option. Journal or share with friends or group.

44

EXERCISE 6: Option #2.
End the relationship or leave the situation.

Sometimes, a positive action may involve a termination. If a situation or relationship has become so unhealthy and destructive that negotiating expectations does not work, it is time to consider terminating it. These are the moments when our "friend anger" is telling us that if we do not get out of whatever is hurting us we will die, physically, mentally or spiritually. After we have exhausted all possibilities, letting go and moving on is the only healthy action left for us.

Look at your situation. How close are you to doing violence to yourself or others? Has your anger augmented because nothing you have tried works? If this is so, it may be time to channel the energy of your anger positively by letting go and moving on. Redirect all the energy that you are wasting in hating or dreaming of revenge, into healing yourself.

At this point a new element enters the equation: forgiveness. Termination can only be positive if the letting go is authentic. For this to happen you need to forgive the person or group that you feel has caused your grief.

Because the concept of forgiveness can be very misunderstood, I am offering some definitions that will help you understand the true meaning of forgiveness .

☹ Forgiveness is not...

1. Denying your hurt.

2. Excusing unjust behaviors. There are inexcusable destructive behaviors: emotional and physical abuse, economic exploitation, racism, or any denial of human rights. To excuse such behaviors is to tolerate and condone them, but by forgiving you render them powerless to destroy you.

3. Putting yourself in dangerous or harmful situations.

4. Forgetting. There are brutalities that must not be forgotten if you are to avoid replaying them. They can, nonetheless, be forgiven.

5. Putting the other person on probation or waiting impatiently for some evidence that they merit your clemency. Then if the person does not measure up to your expectations, the gift of forgiveness is withdrawn. This will be a pseudo-letting go that will not help you in any way.

☺ Forgiveness is…

1. Making a conscious choice to release the offender from the sentence of your judgment. It is a choice to let go of your desire to get even and seek revenge. By doing this, you begin to move from the place of hurt to a place of new life and new beginnings.

2. Breaking the power that the actual wound has to hold you trapped in continual replay of the event, with all the resentment that each remembrance makes fresh. In this sense, forgiveness frees the forgiver!

3. Forgiving even if the offending parties have not asked for forgiveness. Actually, you may not even need to tell them that you have forgiven them.

4. Not to be mistaken for reconciliation! They are different things! The gift of forgiveness will always feel incomplete if it does not result in reconciliation. Forgiveness opens the door to reconciliation, but does not guarantee it!

5. Accepting that reconciliation cannot take place if the other party does not want it, but even if it happens things can never be "the way they were before": they can be better or nothing at all. Both options are possible and acceptable.

6. Both a decision and a process. Thus, it takes time, and it cannot be rushed!

Remember that holding grudges is like taking poison in the hope that it will kill the offender. It is like acid eating away at the peace within us. I believe that the inability to forgive eventually becomes its own kind of hell.

Questions to consider:

- Do you think that termination is your best option?

- Who do you need to forgive? A person? An institution? Your family? The church?

- At this point all you need is the decision to forgive. This is the first step in a long process of healing and wholeness.

- Are you ready? If so, what steps do you personally need to take?

I suggest that you share your decision with a trusted friend or a spiritual companion.

You can also journal and write a letter to the offender sharing your hurt. You may even allow this letter to be answered (by yourself in your journal). Neither letter is to be mailed, but it is meant to help you deal with your feelings openly.

Keep in mind that sometimes, we may need professional assistance to help us with this process of healing.

EXERCISE 7: Option #3.
Become an agent of change.

Anger can also give us the necessary impetus to effect change. In the presence of injustice, abuse, dis-
crimination, racism, exploitation, violation of human
rights and other personal and social evils that plague
our world today we get angry. At least I hope we do! If
these behaviors do not stir any emotions in us it may be
because we are totally self-involved or perhaps dead.

As a Christian, the Gospel urges me to be angry at
injustices and disgusted with all that is wrong with our
society today. I believe that anger is an integral part of
full Christian living and it cannot be dismissed as irrel-
evant or undesirable in a "religious" context. Human
beings have a capacity for moral outrage in the face of
injustices, and this outrage is not optional for the fol-
lowers of Christ. It is the energy of this emotion that
can lead us to improve society in a non-violent way.

Even if you are not a religious person, you can draw
from the wisdom of the prophetic tradition of both
Jews and Christians to guide you in this path.

In the Judeo-Christian Scriptures (Old Testament),
the emotion of anger is mentioned frequently, both
among people and between God and humans. Christians believe that they are in a Covenant relationship
with God, and that just like in any other relationship,
there are disagreements and unmet expectations. The
frustrations of the people are especially captured in the
psalms, one hundred and fifty prayer-songs collected
in a single book called the Psalter and written around
the 10th Century B.C.E.

Consider the following psalms. What do they say to you?

"To you, O Lord, I call… do not refuse to hear me…"
Psalm 28.

"O that you would kill the wicked, O God… Do I not hate those who hate you, O Lord? And do I not loathe those who rise up against you? I hate them with perfect hatred…" Psalm 139.

"Guard me, O Lord, from the hands of the wicked... Let burning coals fall on them! Let them be flung into pits, no more to rise!" Psalm 140.

Do they sound angry to you? It is the anger of a people who felt abandoned by God or that their enemies prospered and they did not. They expressed their feelings freely to God and their prayers covered the full range of human emotions: sorrow, pain, gratitude, petition, joy, but in all of them the confidence and trust in God's goodness always comes through.

If you are considering using option #3 to deal with your anger positively, praying the psalms will be helpful.

Anger was also expressed by the prophets of Israel and by Jesus Christ. When the risen Jesus appeared to his disciples, he greeted them with the word Shalom, peace. Often, this peace has been interpreted as, "being nice", "not getting angry", or "avoiding conflict at all cost". Nothing can be more remote from the true meaning of Shalom. Shalom means unity, peace, integrity, harmony and justice, and we all know that these things do not come easily.

When a person's or a society's shalom is endangered, only the energy of our moral outrage can move us out of our narrow comfort zone to take a prophetic stance. This was the anger of the prophets of Israel when the people failed to "do justice, and to love kindness" (Micah 6:8); when they oppressed their workers, did not share their bread with the hungry, neglected the widow, the orphans and the homeless, or did not welcome the alien (Isaiah 58). Their words were harsh and angry, very angry, and were spoken in the name of God! This is not a "negative" or "sinful" emotion; it may feel uncomfortable, but it is holy!

Jesus also got angry. When he went to Jerusalem to celebrate the Passover, "in the temple he found people selling cattle, sheep, and doves, and the money changers seated at their tables. Making a whip of cords, he drove all of them out of the temple, both the sheep and the cattle. He also poured out the coins of the money changers and overturned their tables. He told those who were selling… 'Take these things out of here! Stop making my Father's house a marketplace'." (John 2:13-16). Jesus' anger surely affected change, but without causing harm to anyone or spending the rest of his days seeking revenge.

On another occasion, he entered the synagogue on a sabbath and "a man was there who had a withered hand. All present watched Jesus to see whether he would cure him on the sabbath, so they might accuse him... He looked around at them with anger; he was grieved at their hardness of heart and said to the man, 'Stretch out your hand.' He stretched it out, and his hand was restored." (Mark 3:1-6). This time, the energy of just anger was channeled into healing!

Do you think that the root of your anger is injustice? Do you feel called to become an agent of change?

(Before you take any action, make sure that you are not having unrealistic expectations. Life is not an utopia and people and structures are imperfect. You cannot apply this option to any small situation that does not suit you. Here you are looking at actions that go directly against your moral values and the dignity of all human beings.)

Is there an unjust situation that needs to be exposed or corrected? Are you the person to do it? Can you do it in a non-violent way?

If you answered yes to these questions, I would like to give you some advice:

- Do not expect to be liked and praised by everyone. Most people feel threatened by prophets, messiahs and "Quixotes".

- Do not build for yourself a new set of unrealistic expectations, such as, "I will be able to right all wrongs and rid the world of evil!" You are going to be disappointed and frustrated all over again.

- Do not try to pray anger away! Christian prayer includes sharing your emotions openly and honestly with your God. If you are a Christian, remember that there is a difference between the feeling of anger and the sin of anger. The Letter to the Ephesians tells us, "Be angry but do not sin; do not let the sun go down on your anger…" (4:26).

- Avoid "chronic" anger. Remember that you cause your own anger and in this case, to be effective, you need to act in a non-violet way. Do not give anyone the power to upset you. Think of the prophets of Israel, Gandhi, Martin Luther King, Rosa Parks, Oscar Romero, Nelson Mandela, Dorothy Day, Jimmy Carter and so many other "angry" people who managed to channel their frustration in a positive non-violent way for the good of their communities.

Spend time reflecting, praying, and asking for advice from trusted friends and relatives. If you have followed the process suggested in this book in a group setting, share with your partner or group members what you feel called to do. Listen to their opinions, value their judgments, and if you are a person of faith, pray at all times!

Chapter Four

Taking action

I know three types of people:
Those who watch things happen.
Those who do not let things happen.
Those who make things happen.

By now you know that you belong to the third group: "Those people who make things happen."

You have spent a significant amount of time reflecting on your anger, its causes, and its untapped positive energy. The time for action is here!

You have followed the three steps of social analysis, "to see, to judge and to act." They have assisted you throughout this process, and by the time you moved through the third step and were ready for action, I suggested three possible ways to channel your anger constructively. Whether you chose option #1: to re-evaluate your expectations; option #2: to terminate the relationship; or option #3: to become an agent of change, you are already on the way to positive action.

The following suggestions will help you, not only to continue this process, but to serve as a guide the next time you get angry. They will be your reminders that it is in your power to prevent frustration and anger from becoming violent behaviors.

1.- Be aware and accept your feelings.

2.- Remember that feelings are neither good nor bad, and that anger as a human emotion is under your conscious control.

3.- Anger is your internal response to a perceived frustration, hurt or injustice. The same stimulus will cause different reactions in other people. Thus, you are the author of your own anger and are capable of dealing with it.

4.- Most anger arises out of intimate and significant relationships, but it could also spring from professional or ecclesial situations in which there is interdependence.

5.- Try to pay attention and listen to your feelings of frustration before they turn into anger.

6.- Do not be so afraid of getting angry that you allow anger to control you.

7.- Understand that your anger may be caused by the memory of something unresolved that happened some time ago.

8.- Follow the steps of social analysis (Chapter 3, page 32) to identify the causes of your anger. Once you identify them, discern whether you need to change your expectations, terminate something, or become an agent of change.

9.- Try to prioritize your expectations. Do not give the same importance to everything. For example:

"People must always be on time."

"Human rights must be respected."

"Children should not be so noisy in church."

"I will not tolerate domestic violence."

"My new car must be red."

Be selective with the situations that you allow to make you angry. Remember that you create your own anger. If you put the blame on other people or situations you will feel powerless and frustrated.

10.- Do not displace your anger towards people who have not done anything to you.

11.- Learn to express your feelings without offending, blaming or attacking others.

12.- Consider that most people act badly out of ignorance or emotional upset and rarely out of malice.

13.- Do not exaggerate or "dramatize" your frustration. Try to stay close to reality.

14.- Be aware of "chronic" anger. People who are always angry live in a hell.

15.- Be nice to yourself. Do things that promote your human and spiritual growth.

16.- When you decide not to express your anger, it will help to release its energy physically through non-violent activities such as walking, jogging, cleaning, sports, cooking, etc. I personally do not like the option of hitting pillows or punching bags. These activities may provide a temporary relief from pent-up anger, but in the long run the more violence you express the more violent you feel.

17.- Other forms of channeling your energy physically are: meditation, prayer, relaxation techniques, listening to music or watching a movie.

18.- Stay open to forgiveness and if possible to reconciliation.

19.- "Do not let the sun go down on your anger." *Ephesians 4:26.*

20.- If you begin to experience anger again, or the desire for vengeance or retaliation, go back to the process outlined in this book.

Shalom

Journal Pages